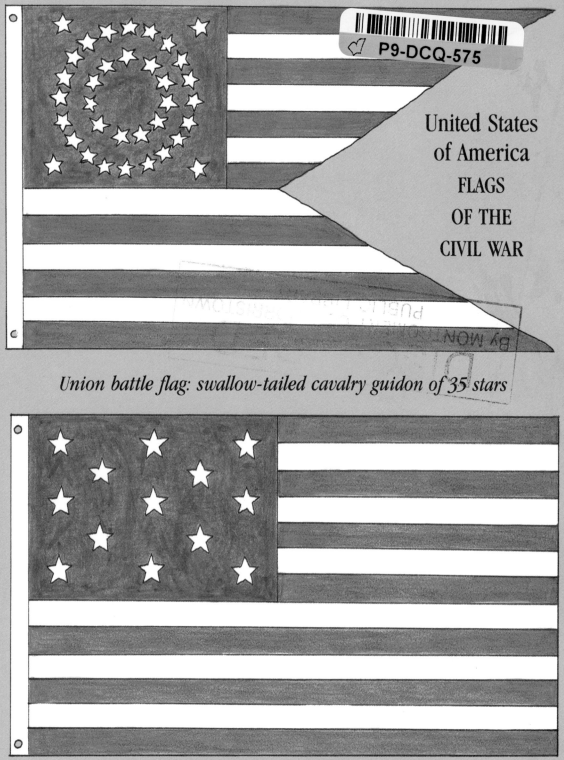

United States
of America
FLAGS
OF THE
CIVIL WAR

Union battle flag: swallow-tailed cavalry guidon of 35 stars

"The Old Flag": "Stars and Stripes" of 13 stars,
used often in Civil War and a favorite of Union troops

Barbara Frietchie

SEPT. 10, 1862

by
John Greenleaf Whittier
illustrated by
Nancy Winslow Parker

Greenwillow Books, New York

ACKNOWLEDGMENTS

Grateful acknowledgment is made to the following for their help in the research
for this work: Angie Brosius and Velma Defibaugh (librarians), and Phyllis Knill of the
Frederick County Historical Society, Frederick, Maryland □ Wanda Dowell, Director, and
Susan Cumbey, Curator, Fort Ward Museum, Alexandria, Virginia □ Michael A. Lynn, Director,
The Stonewall Jackson House, Lexington, Virginia □ Rebecca Ebert, Archivist/Librarian;
Ben Ritter, Reference Assistant; Lisa Whetzel, Archives Assistant; Donna Hughes, Children's
Librarian, The Handley Library, Winchester, Virginia □ Sarah Huggins, Reference Librarian,
Virginia State Library and Archives, Richmond, Virginia □ Private Jim Howard, Corporal
Wayne Smith, and Private Mark Thorpe of Company G, 12th Regiment, Virginia Infantry,
"Richmond Greys"; Private A. Millman, 42nd Virginia Infantry □ Alice Cronin, Librarian,
Point Pleasant, New Jersey □ Ruth Clark Stauffer, Shirley, New York □
Margaret Garrett, Washington, DC.

Watercolors, colored pencils, and a black pen were used for the full-color art.
The text type is Garamond Light Condensed

Printed in Singapore by Tien Wah Press   First Edition   10 9 8 7 6 5 4 3 2 1

Library of Congress Cataloging-in-Publication Data

Whittier, John Greenleaf, 1807-1892.
Barbara Frietchie / by John Greenleaf Whittier;
pictures by Nancy Winslow Parker.
p.   cm.
Summary: An illustrated edition of the poem describing Barbara Fritchie's
dramatic stand with the Union flag against the rebel troops invading her town.
ISBN 0-688-09829-0. ISBN 0-688-09830-4 (lib. bdg.)
1. Fritchie, Barbara, 1766-1862—Juvenile poetry.
2. United States—History—Civil War, 1861-1865—Juvenile poetry.
3. Children's poetry, American. [1. Fritchie. Barbara, 1766-1862—Poetry.
2. United States—History—Civil War, 1861-1865—Poetry. 3. American poetry.
4. Narrative poetry.]   I. Parker, Nancy Winslow, ill.
II. Title. PS3256.A1 1992 811'.3—dc20 90-41755 CIP AC

For my grandfather
Linden James Parker,
Civil War veteran

THE SETTING
Frederick, Maryland, September 1862

*I*n 1862 the United States was in the second year of the Civil War. Abraham Lincoln was President. Maryland, a border state, was held by a federal marshal. The citizens of its second largest city, Frederick, were evenly split between loyalty to the Union and sympathy for the South. One citizen, Barbara Fritchie, 95 years old and the widow of a glovemaker, was fiercely loyal to the Union.

General Robert E. Lee was commander of the Confederate Army of Northern Virginia. His army of 30,000 men, who had been bivouacked outside town, broke camp on September 10 and marched through Frederick on their way to the Battle of Antietam at Sharpsburg.

Thomas Jonathan "Stonewall" Jackson, one of Lee's ablest generals, was also with the Confederate Army when it marched through Frederick. His troops, too, would confront the Union Army at Sharpsburg.

Major General George B. McClellan was commander of 70,000 Union troops of the Army of the Potomac. He would lead them against Lee's and Jackson's forces at Sharpsburg.

A person who watched the Confederate troops march through Frederick on September 10 reported a motley army covered in dirt and filth. Some soldiers had no shoes. The eyewitness said that it took sixteen hours for the entire army of about 55,000 men to pass through the deserted streets—about 4,000 soldiers per hour.

It was on that day that Barbara Fritchie is said to have waved a Union flag at General Stonewall Jackson as his troops marched by her house on West Patrick Street, and it was this event that John Greenleaf Whittier wrote about in his poem "Barbara Frietchie." (Whittier used the German spelling of her name.) However, an officer on General Jackson's staff wrote, "As for Barbara Fritchie, we did not pass her house. There was an old woman of that name in Frederick in her 96th year and bed-ridden. She never saw Stonewall Jackson and he never saw her. I was with him every minute while he was in town, and nothing like the patriotic incident so graphically described by Mr. Whittier in his poem ever occurred."

The Battle of Antietam at Sharpsburg marked the bloodiest single day of the Civil War. On September 17 the battle raged around the little town and along Antietam Creek. At the end of the day it was apparent that McClellan had badly mauled Lee, but he did not press his advantage by calling up his reserves of 24,000 fresh troops, so Lee was able to escape into Virginia. The losses to both sides were staggering. The Union lost 12,410 men; the Confederate losses were 13,724.

Whittier's poem tells us about just one day in a city in the path of the Civil War.

N. W. PARKER

MANTOLOKING, NJ, 1991

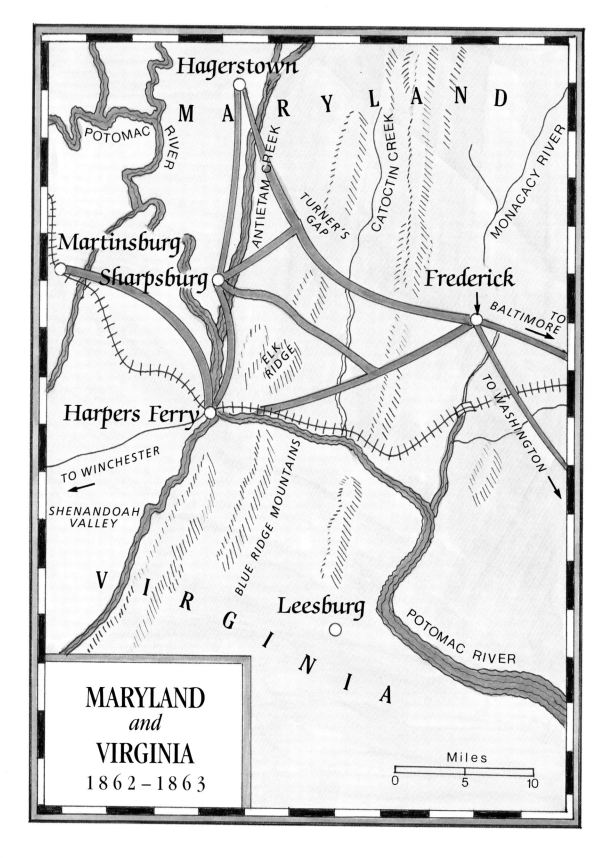

Hagerstown

M A R Y L A N D

POTOMAC RIVER

ANTIETAM CREEK

TURNER'S GAP

CATOCTIN CREEK

MONOCACY RIVER

Martinsburg

Sharpsburg

ELK RIDGE

Frederick

TO BALTIMORE

TO WASHINGTON

Harpers Ferry

TO WINCHESTER

SHENANDOAH VALLEY

BLUE RIDGE MOUNTAINS

Leesburg

V I R G I N I A

POTOMAC RIVER

MARYLAND
and
VIRGINIA
1862 – 1863

Miles

0   5   10

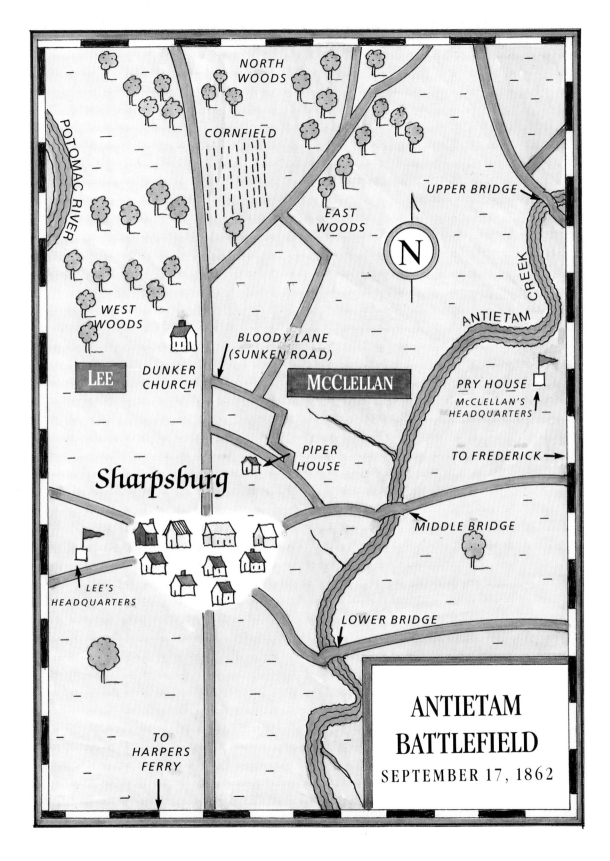

Flag of the State of Maryland,
showing the coats of arms of
the Calverts and the Crosslands

Up from the meadows rich with corn,
Clear in the cool September morn,
The clustered spires of Frederick stand
Green-walled by the hills of Maryland.

Round about them orchards sweep,
Apple and peach tree fruited deep,
Fair as a garden of the Lord,
To the eyes of the famished rebel horde,

On that pleasant morn of the early fall
When Lee marched over the mountain wall—
Over the mountains, winding down,
Horse and foot into Frederick town.

Forty flags with their silver stars,
Forty flags with their crimson bars,

Flapped in the morning wind; the sun
Of noon looked down, and saw not one.

Up rose old Barbara Frietchie then,
Bowed with her fourscore years and ten;
Bravest of all in Frederick town,
She took up the flag the men hauled down;

In her attic-window the staff she set,
To show that one heart was loyal yet.

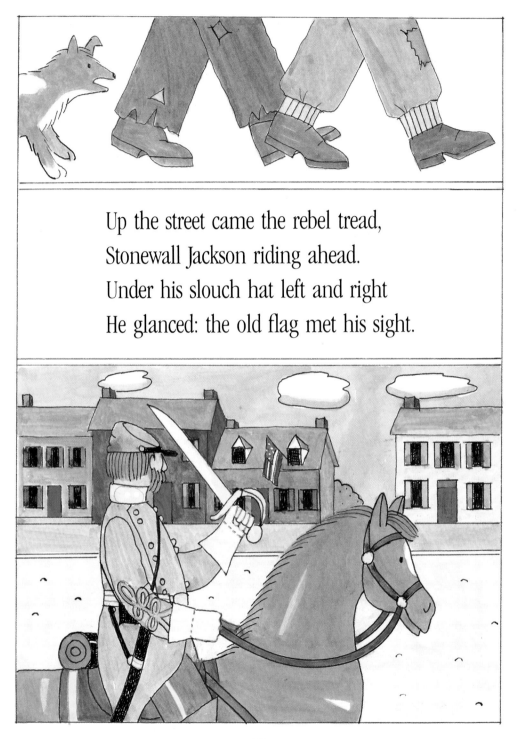

Up the street came the rebel tread,
Stonewall Jackson riding ahead.
Under his slouch hat left and right
He glanced: the old flag met his sight.

"Halt!"—the dust-brown ranks stood fast;
"Fire!"—out blazed the rifle-blast.

It shivered the window, pane and sash;
It rent the banner with seam and gash.

Quick, as it fell, from the broken staff
Dame Barbara snatched the silken scarf;

She leaned far out on the window-sill,
And shook it forth with a royal will.

"Shoot, if you must, this old gray head,
But spare your country's flag," she said.

A shade of sadness, a blush of shame,
Over the face of the leader came;
The nobler nature within him stirred
To life at that woman's deed and word:

"Who touches a hair of yon gray head
Dies like a dog! March on!" he said.

All day long through Frederick street
Sounded the tread of marching feet;

All day long that free flag tost
Over the heads of the rebel host.

Ever its torn folds rose and fell
On the loyal winds that loved it well;
And through the hill-gaps sunset light
Shone over it with a warm good-night.

Barbara Frietchie's work is o'er,
And the rebel rides on his raids no more.
Honor to her! and let a tear
Fall, for her sake, on Stonewall's bier.

Over Barbara Frietchie's grave,
Flag of freedom and union wave!
Peace and order and beauty draw
Round thy symbol of light and law;
And ever the stars above look down
On thy stars below in Frederick town.

Campaign Medal
THE CIVIL WAR
1861–1865
*"With malice towards none,
with charity for all"*

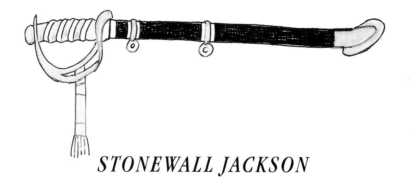

STONEWALL JACKSON

Thomas Jonathan "Stonewall" Jackson was born on January 21, 1824, in Clarksburg, Virginia (now West Virginia). He was an orphan and poorly educated in country schools. He went to the U.S. Military Academy at West Point, where he struggled to pass the tests to stay in the Academy. He slowly improved with time and graduated in 1846. He served in the Mexican War, at various forts in the West, and in Florida fighting the Seminole Indians. In 1851, he resigned his commission in the U.S. Army to teach at Virginia Military Academy, where he stayed for ten years.

At the outbreak of the Civil War, Jackson was appointed a colonel in the Confederate infantry and ordered to Harpers Ferry, where he organized the famous Stonewall Brigade. He was appointed a Brigadier General in 1861 and participated in many of the first battles of the war: the First Battle of Bull Run, the Shenandoah Valley Campaign, the Seven Days Battle, Cedar Mountain, the Second Battle of Bull Run (Manassas), Antietam, and Fredericksburg. By 1862, Jackson was a Lieutenant General and commander of the II Corps, Army of Northern Virginia. At Chancellorsville,

General Jackson was at the peak of his success when he was shot by mistake by one of his own men while he was scouting in the dark. On May 10, 1863, he died of pneumonia, a complication from his wound. His last words were, "Let us cross over the river and rest under the shade of the trees."

Jackson was six feet tall and weighed 175 pounds. He was one of the South's greatest and most-loved generals. His body was taken by special train to Richmond, where he lay in state in the Governor's Mansion, "the coffin-lid having been raised to show the person of the dead; a wreath of laurel was laid upon the breast and around the coffin was wrapped the snow-white banner of the Confederate States."* The next day the coffin was borne to the State Capitol. Along the procession route from Governor's Mansion to Capitol, men and women openly wept. "Such public grief had not been displayed since the death of Washington."*

On Friday, May 15, General Jackson was buried in the village cemetery in Lexington, Virginia.

N.W.P.

Stonewall Jackson: A Military Biography by John Esten Cooke (1876).

JOHN GREENLEAF WHITTIER

John Greenleaf Whittier, an American poet and Quaker, was born in East Haverhill, Massachusetts, in 1807. He grew up on a farm and for a year attended school. After that, he educated himself by reading, especially reading poetry and particularly the poems of Robert Burns. Whittier was an editor on a Boston newspaper and was elected to the Massachusetts legislature. When he became an abolitionist, his political career was cut short, so he turned to writing full time.

Whittier's first book, *Legends of New England in Prose and Verse*, was published in 1831. His poetry can be divided into three periods: the early romantic poems; the militant Quaker works on antislavery; and the later poems devoted to nature. His greatest poem is considered to be "Snow Bound." He also edited the *Journal of John Woolman* (1774), the famous Quaker abolitionist from New Jersey.

Whittier's poem "Barbara Frietchie" was first published in the *Atlantic Monthly* in 1863. He had heard thirdhand about the Fritchie–Jackson incident. By the time he learned the whole story, the facts had been sorely muddled. As soon as the poem was published, people began to dispute its historical accuracy. Many believed that Barbara Fritchie's flag-waving at General Jackson was confused with her reported flag-waving two days later at the Union troops led by General Jesse Reno, who also marched by her house on their way to the front. In defense of his work, the poet wrote in a letter to the *Century Magazine*:

> "The poem of Barbara Frietchie was written in good faith. The story was no invention of mine. It came to me from sources which I regard as entirely reliable; it has been published in newspapers, and had gained public credence in Washington and Maryland before my poem was written....
>
> John G. Whittier
Amesbury, 6 Mo. 10, 1886 "

John Greenleaf Whittier died at the age of 85, a much honored American poet.

N.W.P.

Confederate
States
of America
FLAGS
OF THE
CIVIL WAR

Confederate battle flag, September 1861

First national flag: "Stars and Bars,"
first used March 4, 1861; flown at Fort Sumter